TELL ME
QUICKLY

Short Lessons Learned
Through Pain and Recovery

WRITTEN BY
ASHLEY WOODS

To request permissions, please contact the publisher at awoodswriting@gmail.com.

Paperback:
Thirteen-digit ISBN: 978-0-578-85129-7
Ten-digit ISBN: 0-578-85129-6

Ebook:
Thirteen-digit ISBN: 978-1-7367925-0-6
Ten-digit ISBN: 1-7367925-0-4

Library of Congress Control Number: 2021905370

Printed in the United States of America.
Published in Nashville, TN.

Cover and Interior Design by Tami Boyce (tamiboyce.com)

To Tyler, Beau and Zeke. I love you.

PREFACE

I love to write, but I'm also a full-time working mom with two little kids. Seeking to use my gifts in a manageable way, I started writing short poems to capture lessons learned in my pain, healing and recovery.

As I wrote and shared with others, I found that these writings were as helpful to others as they've been to me. This book is birthed out of a desire to help others, release truth and give God glory.

ACKNOWLEDGEMENTS

Thank you to the people who have worked directly with me on this book to bring it to fruition: Tyler, Debbie, Rachel, Vickie, Barbara, Chandalee, Allison, Adam, Tami, Tara and Emily. I'd also like to thank every single person I've encountered in recovery for helping me grow up and stay grown up.

INTRODUCTION

Traumas as a child left me empty and broken, and I turned to the world to meet needs only God could meet. While mine is a story of pain, it's also a story of ongoing redemption.

In some of my most desperate times, I longed for someone to offer me immediate help and direction. I wanted someone to share the things that I'm sharing in this book. I wished someone would *Tell Me Quickly*.

TABLE OF CONTENTS

PROLOGUE

My dad was a published author

Whose writings wrecked hearts.

I'm here to use those gifts

To mend them.

-A. Woods

HEALING TRAUMA

You cannot heal trauma without talking.

Suppressed memories = trauma untold

Trauma untold = unwanted behaviors

Unwanted behaviors = unwanted consequences

And, if you're fortunate...

Unwanted consequences = point of desperation

Point of desperation = talking

Talking = trauma told

Trauma told = healing

You cannot heal trauma without talking.

-A. Woods

SELF-SABOTAGE

People will self-destruct

When their insides are screaming "help"

But their outsides don't know how

To let the voice out.

-A. Woods

INNER CHILD WORK

PART OF ME

WAS FROZEN IN TIME

SO I TRAVELED BACK

AND CARRIED HER OUT.

-A. WOODS

VULNERABLE

HEALING DOESN'T COME FROM
ONE BIG DISPLAY OF HONESTY
BUT CONTINUOUS MOMENTS
OF VULNERABILITY.

-A. WOODS

REAL STRENGTH

Every tear held in
Made me weaker.
Every tear let out
Made me stronger.

-A. Woods

BREATHE

Trauma dumping
Is anxious.
Trauma telling
Is healing.

-A. Woods

BRAVE

It takes self-esteem
To have boundaries.
It takes courage
To communicate them.

-A. Woods

RISKS

If I don't take risks,
I stay at the same level
Of intimacy and healing
As yesterday.

-A. Woods

PLAY FAIR

Proverbs warns men

Of the harlot in the streets.

Should we not also

Warn the women

Of the uncontrolled men?

-A. Woods

THE WORLD IS YOUR OYSTER

In sickness,

I love one thing.

In health,

I love many things.

-A. Woods

NOT ANXIOUS

I can rest.

I can change my mind.

I don't have to be perfect.

Because I'm not anxious anymore.

-A. Woods

FIVE-YEAR-OLD ME

SOMETIMES WHEN I THINK ABOUT LOVING MYSELF
I DON'T THINK I'M WORTH IT.
BUT I THINK FIVE-YEAR-OLD ME IS WORTH IT
AND SHE'S STILL IN THERE
SO NOW WHEN I THINK ABOUT LOVING MYSELF
I JUST THINK ABOUT LOVING THAT LITTLE GIRL.

-A. WOODS

SHAME

A life of toxic shame
Is full of big highs and big lows.
A life of little shame
Is level and consistent.

-A. Woods

TRUST

Unhealed,

I don't trust.

Healed,

I trust.

-A. Woods

LET GO

It was hard
To walk away
Because I was always
Holding too tightly.

-A. Woods

ANGER

Anger doesn't always look
like red faces & fist fights.
Anger can look like depression.
Anger can look like self-harm.
Anger can look like addiction.

-A. Woods

CHANGE

Not everyone

Is ready for change

Because not everyone

Sees the need.

-A. Woods

A POEM TO GOD

How needy I must be
To accept the things You hand me.
How poor I must be
To consider wealth differently.
How humbled I must be
To follow Your decree.

-A. Woods

PURPOSE

I'll be whatever I want

Changed to

I'll be whatever you want

Changed to

I'll be whatever God made me to be.

-A. Woods

LUST

Lust kills love
So kill the lust
And love reappears.

-A. Woods

MY CHILDREN

I could stay a victim forever
But I'd just create more victims
And I'm in the business
Of making victors.

-A. Woods

SELF-WORK

The more I worked
On my outward appearance
The more I hated myself.
The more I worked
On my inward appearance
The more I loved myself.

-A. Woods

PRIORITIES

I fear people
But I fear God more.

-A. Woods

LIGHT

I KEPT IT IN MY HEAD
AND GOT SICK.
I PUT IT IN THE LIGHT
AND GOT WELL.

-A. WOODS

CHILDREN OF NARCISSISTS

You could never love me

But would never let me go

So I had to free myself.

-A. Woods

NO SECRETS

A BAD MAN

TOLD ME TO KEEP SECRETS

BUT I DON'T KEEP SECRETS

THAT PROTECT BAD BEHAVIOR.

-A. WOODS

LOVED FOR NOTHING

All the love I got

From serving

Accomplishing

And Working

Was never enough

Because what I needed

Was to be loved for nothing.

-A. Woods

TEARS

As a child,

I watched

And no tears fell.

As an adult,

I spoke about what I saw

And the tears came.

Tears were always appropriate

Mine were just delayed.

-A. Woods

RELEASE THE DOVES

The doves of my anger, bitterness & resentment

I release in private with few people present.

The doves of my love, joy & hope

I release in public.

Both are beautiful but only one

Is seen as beautiful by all.

-A. Woods

BOUNDARIES BASED ON PROVERBS

THE MOCKER REJECTS EVERYTHING.

[RIGID BOUNDARIES]

THE INEXPERIENCED ACCEPTS EVERYTHING.

[LOOSE BOUNDARIES]

THE SENSIBLE WATCHES THEIR STEPS.

[HEALTHY BOUNDARIES]

-A. WOODS

PROVERBS 30:21-23

PROVERBS SAYS THE EARTH TREMBLES
WHEN AN UNLOVED WOMAN GETS A HUSBAND.
BUT HOW MUCH DOES THE DEVIL TREMBLE
WHEN THAT UNLOVED WOMAN FINDS GOD?

-A. WOODS

PERSPECTIVE

WHEN A PARENT CHOOSES NOT TO STAY

IT HAS EVERYTHING TO DO WITH THE PARENT

AND NOTHING TO DO WITH THE CHILD.

-A. WOODS

BALANCE

Spend time with good people

That keep you from being drug down

By the world

But not so many good people

That you forget

The world needs you.

-A. Woods

HEAL

You won't heal their heart

Until you heal their mind.

-A. Woods

Admit Our Wrongs

Confess your wrongs

To be restored to God

And so Satan

Has nothing left to say.

-A. Woods

PAIN

Pain teaches us.

Pain changes us.

Pain prunes us.

Pain reminds us.

-A. Woods

KEEP GOING

If it still hurts,
There's more healing to do.

-A. Woods

ADDICTION

Many of us turn to addiction

Because someone abandoned us.

But every time we turn to addiction

We're abandoning ourselves.

-A. Woods

LET LOVE IN

My unwillingness

To let people love me

Is a reflection

Of my unwillingness

To let God love me.

-A. Woods

REACH

When I got married,

I was so focused on how God

Could use my marriage to reach others

That I missed how much God

Would use my marriage to reach me.

-A. Woods

SELF-PITY

Self-pity

Is misplaced

Self-care.

Find what you actually need.

-A. Woods

HEALING: PARTY OF ONE

THE HARDEST PART OF HEALING

WAS REALIZING

NO ONE COULD DO IT FOR ME.

-A. WOODS

SELF-LOVE

I can receive love.

I don't have to put myself down.

I can eat what I want.

Because I don't hate myself anymore.

-A. Woods

THE EMOTIONALLY UNAVAILABLE

They aren't less intelligent.

They're less engaged.

-A. Woods

MULTIPLY

Lead with strength
To multiply pride.
Lead with weakness
To multiply humility.

-A. Woods

MARRIAGE

Two things I've learned about marriage:

Pursue spiritual intimacy first

And

Do what you can

To help both people feel supported.

-A. Woods

NEW WAYS

I'd rather do good things

Awkwardly

Than bad things

Naturally.

-A. Woods

PROVERBS 26:11

THE DOG RETURNS TO ITS OWN VOMIT

BECAUSE IT STILL NEEDS REMINDING

THAT THERE'S SOMETHING BETTER.

-A. WOODS

HOPE

An unloved beginning
Can have a loved ending.

-A. Woods

70-YEAR-OLD

Even a 70-year-old
has never been 70 before.
We're all just
learning as we go.

-A. Woods

LET THIS GO

People I loved

Pushed me into a pool of loneliness

I sunk in confusion

Reemerged with a vengeance

Until God cut me off

And said

"Let this go

And go do something good."

-A. Woods

CHARACTER DEFECTS

In health, they're strengths.

In sickness, defects.

In God, ashes & crowns to set at His feet.

-A. Woods

GOOD FROM BAD

People pleasing ends
where people disappoint.

-A. Woods

PHILIPPIANS 1:14

LET THE SUFFERING YOU SEE
LEAD TO BOLDNESS FOR GOD.

-A. WOODS

BODY LANGUAGE

An ignorant person's silence

Hurts.

An empathetic person's silence

Heals.

-A. Woods

FOLLOW UP

IF AN INITIAL CONVERSATION SAYS:

"I SEE YOU AND I HEAR YOU."

FOLLOWING UP SAYS:

"I REMEMBER YOU AND I LOVE YOU."

IF AN INITIAL CONVERSATION SAYS:

"HERE'S A PROBLEM AND HERE'S A SOLUTION."

FOLLOWING UP SAYS:

"I CARE ABOUT THE SUCCESS OF THIS."

FOLLOW UP.

-A. WOODS

COMPLACENCY

I shared my faith

Until I looked around and felt too radical.

I shared my Truth

Until I looked around and felt too honest.

So I stopped.

Until I looked around and saw God.

So I repented

And stopped looking around.

-A. Woods

DISCIPLESHIP

Discipleship
At home
Is discipleship
To the world.

-A. Woods

POWER

Refusing to admit

That you had power over me

Left me powerless

But admitting

That you did have power over me

Gave me the power back.

-A. Woods

SELF-CARE

Sometimes I think acting like

I have no needs

Will get me farther

But, in reality,

Taking care of yourself

Is what breeds longevity.

-A. Woods

PARENTING

Every parent has failed.

Every parent does fail.

Every parent will fail.

But another thing I know:

There's no one your child wants more than you.

-A. Woods

LEARNING TO STAY

Unhealed,

I run.

Healed,

I stay.

-A. Woods

HEART OF FLESH

Before God,

I sinned

And felt nothing.

After God,

I sinned

And ached.

-A. Woods

UNMANAGEABLE

Some people won't understand you

And needing them to understand

Is unmanageable.

-A. Woods

NO LOOSE ENDS

I DIDN'T NEED CLOSURE.

I NEEDED ACCEPTANCE.

-A. WOODS

SELF-ESTEEM

Low self-esteem

Looks for safety in others.

High self-esteem

Looks for safety in God.

-A. Woods

2 CORINTHIANS 2:5-8

Discipline must be followed
by an affirmation of love.

-A. Woods

COMMUNITY

I don't just need community.

I need a knowledgeable community.

-A. Woods

ROPE

I TIED A KNOT IN A ROPE

FOR EACH ANXIETY, FEAR & WORRY

THAT WAS IN MY HEART

AND THEN LOOSENED EACH KNOT

AS I RELEASED EACH ANXIETY, FEAR & WORRY

TO GOD IN PRAYER.

IT REMINDED ME

THAT I'M MOST USEFUL

WHEN I'M THE MOST UNDONE.

-A. WOODS

HIS YOKE IS EASY

WE DON'T HAVE TO CARRY PEOPLE'S OPINIONS.
ONLY GOD'S TRUTH.

-A. WOODS

THE CODEPENDENT

Support yourself

The way you support others

And you won't

Resent so much.

-A. Woods

OPEN HANDS

My job is to parent,
Not control.

-A. Woods

FORGIVENESS

My unwillingness

To forgive

Is a reflection

Of my unwillingness

To be forgiven.

-A. Woods

REAL HEALING

I WAS NEVER GOING TO HEAL
UNTIL I LOOKED AT MY PART IN THINGS.

-A. WOODS

NOT INSECURE

I don't feel threatened.

I can receive feedback.

I can let people go

Who don't want me.

Because I'm not insecure anymore.

-A. Woods

PEACE

I KNOW IT WAS A MISTAKE

IF I HAVE UNREST WITH GOD.

I KNOW I DID RIGHT

IF I HAVE PEACE WITH GOD.

-A. WOODS

BELIEVE IN YOURSELF

They didn't believe in me

Until I believed in myself.

-A. Woods

TEACHABLE

In pride,
I'm teachable to few.
In humility,
I'm teachable to many.

-A. Woods

GOD'S LOVE

I DIDN'T KNOW HOW TO LOVE
UNTIL I FOUND GOD'S LOVE.

-A. WOODS

SHAME POEM

Shame, you are accusing,

Refusing

To let go of my heart.

Shame, you are deceiving,

Receiving

The best and worst of me.

Shame, have you met Jesus?

Retrieved us

With holy, perfect flesh.

-A. Woods

HUMILITY

Humility is the perspective
That you & I are equal
And there's something
Bigger than both of us.

-A. Woods

CONNECTION

If ego ↑, then loneliness ↑

If humility ↑, then connection ↑

In my ego, I am unreachable.

In humility, I am reachable.

-A. Woods

PROVERBS 14:14

Where there are no oxen

The stables are clean.

Relationships bring mess

But also a harvest.

-A. Woods

SILENT GEMS

SILENT GEMS ARE PEOPLE

WHO SERVE GOD

NOT THEIR EGOS.

THAT'S WHY

THEY CAN REMAIN SILENT ABOUT IT.

-A. WOODS

GO FOR REAL GOLD

COMPETITION IS EMPTY.

MISSION IS FULFILLING.

-A. WOODS

LEADERSHIP

Under pride,

People grow hopeless.

Under humility,

People grow hopeful.

-A. Woods

PURE LOVE

I LOVE YOU BEST
WHEN I NEED NOTHING FROM YOU.

-A. WOODS

COMEBACK

No matter what you did wrong,

God always offers a comeback story.

Come back

To Him.

-A. Woods

SAFE PLACE

I CAN MAKE MISTAKES.

I CAN SAY WHAT I WANT.

I CAN FEEL ALL THE FEELINGS.

BECAUSE I'M IN MY SAFE PLACE.

-A. WOODS

THE RIGHT INVESTMENTS

Invest in people

That invest in you.

-A. Woods

GRIEF

In health,

Both joy & sorrow

Hold equal weight

In my heart.

-A. Woods

ANGELS & DEMONS

TELL ME YOUR TRAUMAS
AND I'LL KNOW WHERE YOUR PAIN COMES FROM.
TELL ME WHERE YOU'VE SEEN GOD'S GRACE
AND I'LL KNOW WHERE YOUR HOPE COMES FROM.

-A. WOODS

SELFISH AMBITION

I LET GO OF SELFISH AMBITION

WHEN I REALIZED I CANNOT

SINGLE-HANDEDLY MAKE THE WORLD

A BETTER PLACE FOR MY KIDS.

IT TAKES EVERYONE

TO MAKE THE WORLD A BETTER PLACE

SO I WANT EVERYONE TO DO WELL.

-A. WOODS

FREEDOM

REPENTANCE

BRINGS FORGIVENESS

BUT NOT NECESSARILY FREEDOM.

FREEDOM COMES FROM

A RIGHT VIEW OF GOD.

-A. WOODS

HEART GAUGE

I LOOKED AT YOU

AND MY HEART STOPPED BEATING

BECAUSE I STILL NEEDED HEALING.

I LOOKED AT YOU AGAIN

AND MY HEART KEPT BEATING

BECAUSE I HAD HEALED.

-A. WOODS

CHURCH

Three things I've learned about church:

1. Check your expectations at the door

2. If you see something you want done, go do it

And

3. Don't let imperfect Christians
keep you from a perfect God.

-A. Woods

FINAL HEALING

I want you

Changed to

I fear you

Changed to

I hate you

Changed to

I understand you.

-A. Woods

SURRENDER

I can only follow God's will
When I surrender my agenda
Daily.

-A. Woods

REPENTANCE

I FEEL LIGHTER

I SEE CLEARER

WHEN I'M REPENTING.

-A. WOODS

GOD

My biggest regrets
are the things I've done for my own glory.
My biggest successes
are the things I've done for God's glory.
I hope this book brings God glory.

-A. Woods

If you enjoyed this poetry book or it helped you in some way,
please consider leaving an online review
on Amazon or Barnes & Noble.

For more writings from Ashley, check out her other poetry book,
Tell Me Gently, online at Amazon and Barnes & Noble.

You can also find Ashley's short poetry
writings on Instagram @poetry_that_helps.

Made in United States
Orlando, FL
18 January 2022

13678781R00071